NEW

HORIZONS

OXFORD

Secular
SATB unaccompanied

HOWARD SKEMPTON

Poems of Love and War

Composer's note

Poems of Love and War is a sequence of settings of nine poems from 'Viking Poetry of Love and War' by Judith Jesch. The war poems come first and are formal and celebratory, making vivid use of figures of speech known as "kennings". The love poems are more direct, and sometimes playful.

Howard Skempton
October 2019

For more information about the texts, see:
JESCH, Judith, ed., *Viking Poetry of Love and War* (The British Museum Press, 2013).

Poems of Love and War

1. 'The earl bore his banner'

Arnor Thordarson (11th century)
trans. Judith Jesch (b. 1954)

HOWARD SKEMPTON

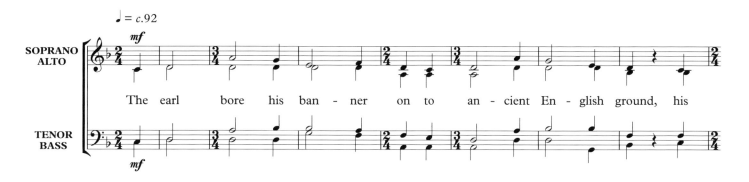

The earl bore his ban-ner on to an-cient En-glish ground, his

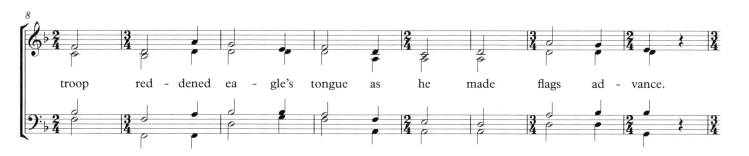

troop red-dened ea-gle's tongue as he made flags ad-vance.

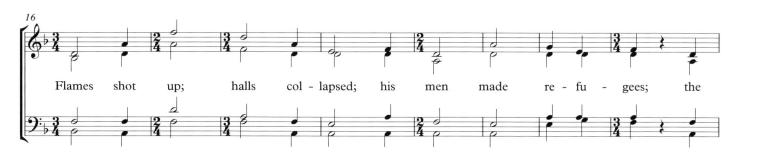

Flames shot up; halls col-lapsed; his men made re-fu-gees; the

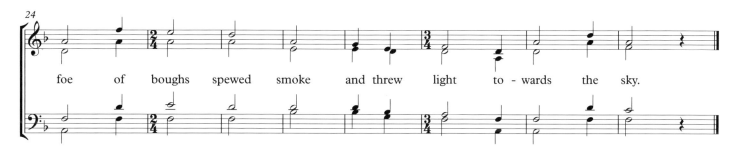

foe of boughs spewed smoke and threw light to-wards the sky.

Duration: 8 mins

Printed in Great Britain

OXFORD UNIVERSITY PRESS, MUSIC DEPARTMENT, GREAT CLARENDON STREET, OXFORD OX2 6DP

2. 'Sword-edges clashed'

Egil Skallagrimsson (10th century)
trans. Judith Jesch

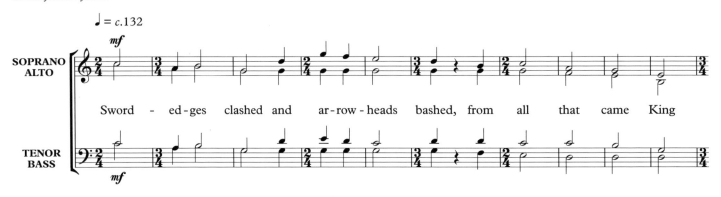

Sword-ed-ges clashed and ar-row-heads bashed, from all that came King

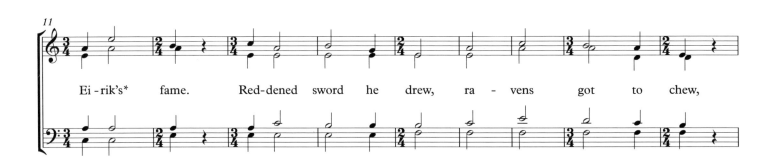

Ei-rik's* fame. Red-dened sword he drew, ra-vens got to chew,

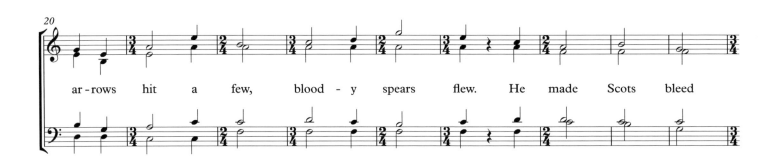

ar-rows hit a few, blood-y spears flew. He made Scots bleed

witch-es' mounts to feed. Na-ri's† sis-ter stood on the ea-gle's food.

* pronounced 'Ayrik's'
† pronounced 'Nahri's'

3. 'Bright sun will become black'

Arnor Thordarson (11th century)
trans. Judith Jesch

Bright sun will be - come black, earth will sink in - to dark sea,

Aus - tri's* bur - den will break, waves will co - ver moun - tains, be -

-fore a bet - ter chief - tain than Thor - finn will be raised in

these isles; may God help that liege of his hall - troop.

* pronounced 'Owstri's'

4. 'Giver of captured gold'

Arnor Thordarson (11th century)
trans. Judith Jesch

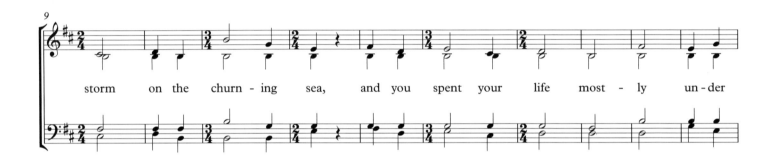

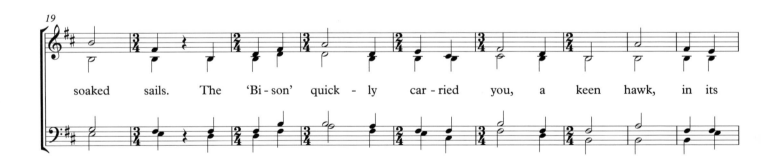

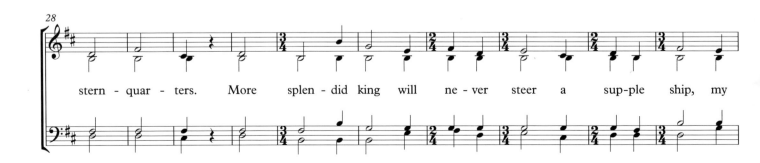

gen - 'rous friend. When the ru – ler ra – ces his sea - skis on the

roll – ing slopes of Me - i – ti,* it seems like an an - gel com-pa - ny

cruis – ing for the Lord of Hea – ven. The spoil – er of the rough

sea's steeds is loved se -cond on - ly to God by the peo – ple of

this na - tion. Your roy - al - ty re - mains for - ev - er.

* pronounced 'Mayti'

5. 'I thought, when I caught sight'

Hallfred Ottarsson (10th century)
trans. Judith Jesch

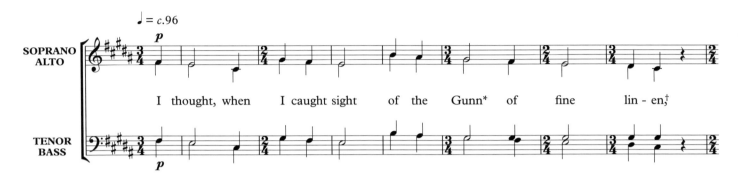

I thought, when I caught sight of the Gunn* of fine lin - en,†

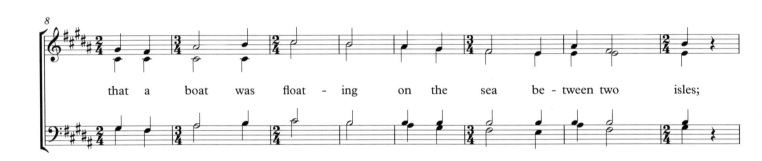

that a boat was float - ing on the sea be - tween two isles;

and the seam - Sa - ga‡ gleamed a - midst the stream of wo - men,

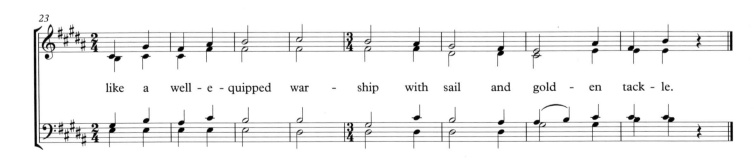

like a well - e - quipped war - ship with sail and gold - en tack - le.

* pronounced 'Goon', with 'oo' as in 'book'
† *Gunn of fine linen* = a kenning for woman, meaning 'headdress-valkyrie'
‡ *seam-Saga* = a kenning for woman. 'Saga' is the name of a goddess, with 'seam' alluding to the textiles she is wearing.

6. 'All the grown girls'

Anonymous (10th century)
trans. Judith Jesch

SOPRANO / ALTO

All the grown girls want-ed to go with In - golf,

All____ the grown girls want-ed to go with In -

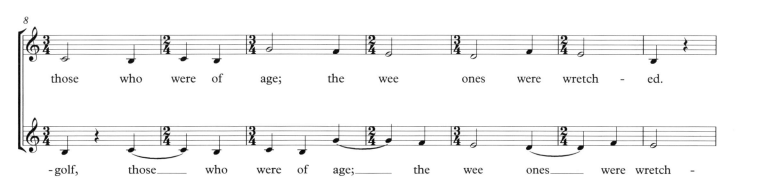

those who were of age; the wee ones were wretch - ed.

-golf, those____ who were of age;____ the wee ones____ were wretch -

'I, too,' said the old wo - man, 'want to go with In - golf, as

-ed. 'I, too,' said the old wo - man, 'want to go with In - golf,

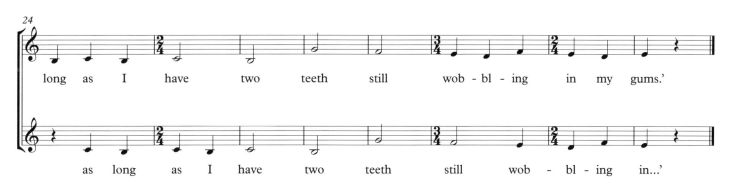

long as I have two teeth still wob - bl - ing in my gums.'

as long as I have two teeth still wob - bl - ing in...'

7. 'In Gymir's gardens'

Anon. (from the *Poetic Edda*)
trans. Judith Jesch

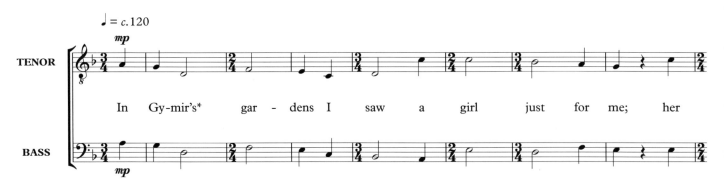

In Gy-mir's* gar - dens I saw a girl just for me; her

arms shone, and from them all the air and all the sea. That

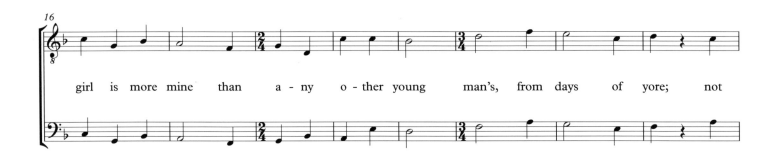

girl is more mine than a - ny o - ther young man's, from days of yore; not

one of the gods or elves want us to be to - ge - ther.

* pronounced 'Gimir's', with 'gi' as in 'gift'

8. 'It's a fact, wise woman'

Rognvald Kali Kolsson, Earl of Orkney (12th century)
trans. Judith Jesch

It's a fact, wise wo-man, that your hair is pret-ti-

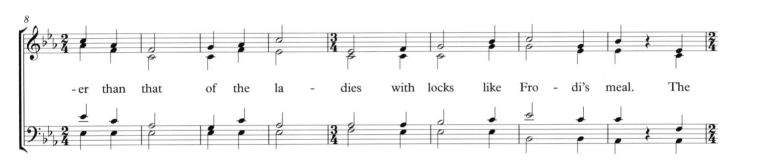

-er than that of the la-dies with locks like Fro-di's meal. The

prop of the hawk-field* lets hair like gold-en silk fall

on-to her shoul-ders; I red-den the ea-gle's claws.

* a kenning for woman

9. 'Praise the day at evening'

Anonymous (from the *Poetic Edda*)
trans. Judith Jesch

Praise the day at eve-ning, the wife when she's cre-ma-ted, a

sword when it's test-ed, a girl when she's mar-ried,

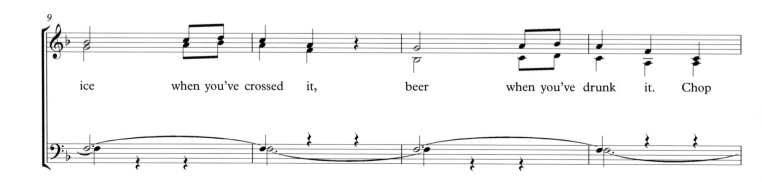

ice when you've crossed it, beer when you've drunk it. Chop

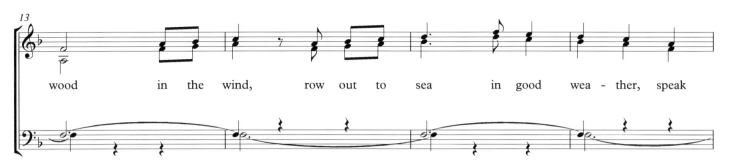

wood in the wind, row out to sea in good wea - ther, speak

to a girl in the dark; the day's eyes are ma - ny; you

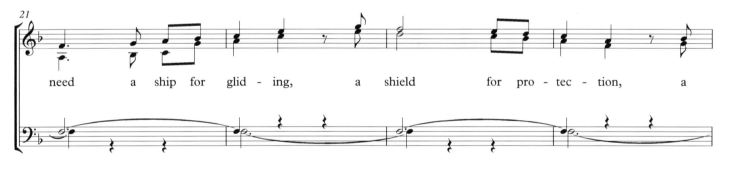

need a ship for glid - ing, a shield for pro - tec - tion, a

sword for strik - ing, a mai - den for kiss - ing.

hum

September 2019

NEW HORIZONS showcases the wealth of exciting, innovative, and occasionally challenging choral music being written today. It encompasses the whole gamut of small-scale choral genres, both secular and sacred, and includes pieces for upper-voice and mixed choirs. With titles by some of the most accomplished choral composers active in the United Kingdom and abroad, the series introduces new repertoire and fresh talent to a broad spectrum of choirs.

Howard Skempton

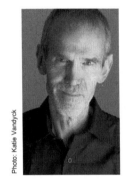

Photo: Katie Vandyck

Born in Chester in 1947, Howard Skempton has worked as a composer, accordionist, and music publisher. Renowned for the distinctive clarity of his musical language, he has composed over 300 pieces, many of which are miniatures for solo piano or accordion. His orchestral and instrumental works have been recorded by, among others, the BBC Symphony Orchestra and Ensemble Bash. In recent years, Skempton has concentrated increasingly on writing vocal and choral music: his choral commissions include works for the BBC Singers and the Belfast Philharmonic Society. CDs of Skempton's choral music—'Ben Somewhen' (NMC D135) and 'The Cloths of Heaven' (DCD34056)—are available on the NMC and Delphian labels.

OXFORD
UNIVERSITY PRESS

www.oup.com

ISBN 978-0-19-353354-7

9 780193 533547